SCHOLAST

MW00446379

Success With

Consonants

New York • Toronto • London • Auckland • Sydney
Mexico City • New Delhi • Hong Kong • Buenos Aires

Teaching *Resources*

State Standards Correlations

To find out how this book helps you meet your state's standards, log on to **www.scholastic.com/ssw**

Written by Robin Wolfe
Cover design by Ka-Yeon Kim-Li
Interior illustrations by Janet Armbrust
Interior design by Quack & Company

ISBN-13 978-0-545-20114-8
ISBN-10 0-545-20114-4

6 7 8 9 10   40   17 16 15 14 13

Introduction

This book is a valuable teaching tool for beginning readers. The activities in it give them practice recognizing the sounds that consonants make at the beginning, in the middle, and at the end of words. They will also find activities that help them learn about special consonants having more than one sound. Rhyming words and silent consonants are included, as well. Children will enjoy completing puzzles, word finds, hidden pictures, and other fun activities as they learn consonant sounds. Understanding phonics is a very important part of learning to read. Equip your children with word attack skills that will help them the rest of their lives!

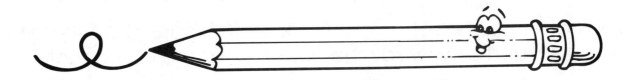

Table of Contents

What Is a Consonant?

Can you say the alphabet? There are 26 letters in the alphabet. Five of the letters are vowels: *A, E, I, O,* and *U.*

All the rest are consonants.

Look at the alphabet below. Mark an *X* through the five vowels: *A, E, I, O,* and *U.* Now say the names of all the consonants.

A B C D E F G H I

J K L M N O P Q

R S T U V W X Y Z

How many consonants are there? _____

Color each balloon that has a consonant in it.

Bobby the Bear

 B *makes the sound you hear at the beginning of the words* **Bobby** *and* **bear**.

Bobby the bear is going shopping for things that begin with **b**. Help Bobby find ten things in this store that begin with **b**. Draw a green circle around each one.

 What insect buzzes around flowers and makes honey? Draw it on another sheet of paper. Tell a friend what you know about this insect.

Doctor Dave

 D *makes the sound you hear at the beginning of the words* **doctor** *and* **Dave**.

Look in Doctor Dave's bag. Color only the pictures that begin with **d**. Put an *X* on the pictures that do not begin with **d**.

 She is another kind of doctor. She works on your teeth. Her job begins with *d*. **Who is she? On another sheet of paper, draw yourself at her office.**

Fancy the Fish

F *makes the sound you hear at the beginning of the words* **fancy** *and* **fish**.

Fancy the fish is blowing bubbles. Draw a bubble around the pictures that begin with **f**. Put an *X* on the pictures that do not begin with **f**.

This word begins with *f*. It names a brave person who saves people when their houses are burning. Who is this person? On another sheet of paper, draw a picture of this person's truck.

Happy the Hippo

➡️ **H** *makes the sound you hear at the beginning of the words* **happy** *and* **hippo**.

Help Happy the hippo find the **h** words. Say the picture in each box. Color only the pictures that begin with **h**.

💡 **This game begins with *h*. One child counts to ten and then tries to find the other children. Do you know what it is? At playtime, play this game with your friends.**

8   Scholastic Success With Consonants

Joe the Janitor

 J *makes the sound you hear at the beginning of the words* **Joe** *and* **janitor**.

Help Joe the janitor find the **j** words. In each trash can, draw a box around two pictures that begin with **j**.

 What kind of candy begins with *j*, **looks like beans, and comes in lots of different colors? Say the answer. On another sheet of paper, draw a glass jar with 21 of these in it. Count carefully! Color them.**

Katie the Kangaroo

 K *makes the sound you hear at the beginning of the words* **Katie** *and* **kangaroo**.

Show Katie the kangaroo how to work this puzzle. Find the puzzle pieces with pictures that begin with **k**. Cut them out. Glue them together on another sheet of paper so that they make the shape of the letter **k**. The pictures that do not begin with **k** will not work in the puzzle.

 This word begins with *k*. **It can mean a young goat, or it can mean a young person. It rhymes with** *lid*. **What is it?**

Name _____

Lazy the Lion

 L *makes the sound you hear at the beginning of the words* **lazy** *and* **lion**.

Help Lazy the lion find a word that begins with **l** to match each picture. Circle the correct word.

lamp clock	zipper lace	tree leaf	ladder hoe
ladybug bee	lake town	dog lamb	hand leg
lightning snow	apple lemon	book letter	lettuce corn
nose lips	lizard goat	worm lobster	log rock

 This word begins with an l. It is a good feeling that you have about the people you like the most. It makes you want to hug someone! What is it? On another sheet of paper, draw or write a list of all the people you feel this way about.

Mike the Mailman

 M *makes the sound you hear at the beginning of the words* **Mike** *and* **mailman**.

Help Mike the mailman sort the mail. Cut out the mail below. If it has a picture on it that begins with **m**, glue it in the bag marked with an **m**. If the picture does not begin with **m**, throw it away.

 I am a woman in your family. I cook for you. I wash your clothes. I take care of you when you are sick. I love you. You call me a name that begins with *m*. Who am I? On another sheet of paper, draw a picture of this person and tell something nice about her.

Nancy the Nurse

 N *makes the sound you hear at the beginning of the words* **Nancy** *and* **nurse**.

After Nancy the nurse gives a shot, she also gives a lollipop to help her young patients feel better. Color the lollipops below that have pictures beginning with **n**.

 This item begins with *n*. It is made of big sheets of paper. It has lots of pictures and words on it. It tells what is happening in the world. Grown-ups like to read it. What is it? Find one of these and look at one page of it. Find words you know. Circle them with a marker. Show a grown-up what you can read!

Patsy the Pig

➡ **P** *makes the sound you hear at the beginning of the words* **Patsy** *and* **pig**.

Help Patsy the pig find the words that
begin with **p**. Use a purple crayon to
write the letter **p** on top of each
picture below that begins with **p**.

 This item is a word that begins with *p*. **It has a head and a tail, but it is not an animal.
It is a copper-colored coin. What is it? Draw it on another sheet of paper, or put one
under the paper and rub over it with a crayon.**

Ricky the Rabbit

 R *makes the sound you hear at the beginning of the words* **Ricky** *and* **rabbit**.

Look at all the fun things that Ricky the rabbit can do. Circle the **r** word that tells what Ricky is doing in each picture.

rest play	swim run	ride hug
rock look	climb rake	stand roll
read sing	rope feed	rip talk
row eat	race walk	sleep rush

 This word begins with *r*. It blasts off into outer space. It orbits Earth. What is it? On another sheet of paper, draw a picture of one that has landed on the moon. Pretend you are an astronaut. Make up a story about your picture.

Silly Sally

S makes the sound you hear at the beginning of the words **silly** *and* **Sally**.

Silly Sally is looking for something that starts with **s**. You can help her find it hidden in the puzzle below. Color each space orange that has a picture in it that begins with **s**. If the picture does not begin with **s**, do not color that space.

 If you take two pieces of bread and put peanut butter on one and jelly on the other, then stick them together, what have you made? It begins with *s*. Pretend you are making one by doing a pantomime.

Tammy the Teacher

 T *makes the sound you hear at the beginning of the words* **Tammy** *and* **teacher**.

1. Trace over the letter in each row.

2. Color the pictures in each row that begin with *t*.

   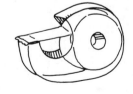

 This item begins with *t*. **Campers sleep in it. What is it?**

Vicki's Vacation

  V *makes the sound you hear at the beginning of the words* **Vicki** *and* **vacation**.

Vicki is going on a vacation. Help Vicki load her van with things that start with **v**. Draw a line from the **v** words to the van.

💡 **It can be a mountain. When it gets very, very hot inside, lava comes out of the top and runs down the sides. It begins with the letter *v*. What is it? On another sheet of paper, draw one and color it.**

Willy the Worm

 W *makes the sound you hear at the beginning of the words* **Willy** *and* **worm**.

In the story below, there are 11 words that begin with **w**. Draw a wiggly line under each one.

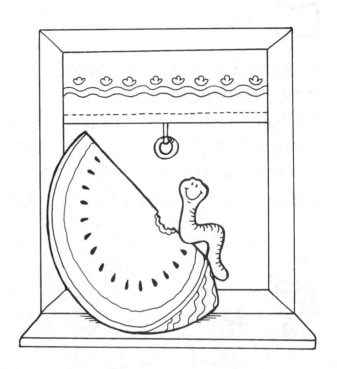

   Willy the worm felt hungry. He

wanted something to eat. He saw

a watermelon in the window.

He climbed up on the wagon.

He wiggled up the wall. Then he

took a bite. Wow! It was wonderful!

Now, circle each word that you underlined in the puzzle. The words go across and down.

x	w	i	g	g	l	e	d	v	t
w	a	t	e	r	m	e	l	o	n
o	g	e	k	p	r	s	b	y	w
w	o	r	m	h	f	l	x	z	i
k	n	c	w	i	n	d	o	w	l
g	v	w	a	n	t	e	d	a	l
u	w	h	s	r	z	q	g	l	y
w	o	n	d	e	r	f	u	l	a

 This begins with *w*. **You cannot see it, but you can feel it. Sometimes you can hear it blowing. It makes the trees sway. What is it? Now, roll up a very small piece of paper and put it on your desk. Blow on it. What happens? Why?**

Yolanda's Yearbook

 Y *makes the sound you hear at the beginning of the words* **Yolanda** *and* **yearbook**.

Yolanda got a yearbook at school today. It has funny pictures in it. Which pictures go together? Draw lines to match the pictures in Yolanda's yearbook. The words in each picture begin with **y**. Can you say them?

 This word begins with *y***. It is one way to answer a question. When you say it, you nod your head up and down. What word is it? Now play this game. Take turns acting out these words without saying anything: No. I don't know. Who me? Stop! Come here. Be quiet. Too loud!**

Zachary the Zebra

 Z *makes the sound you hear at the beginning of the words* **Zachary** *and* **zebra**.

Zachary the zebra is lost! Help him find his way back to the zoo. Circle only the things that begin with **z**. Connect them to the **z**'s you find along the way.

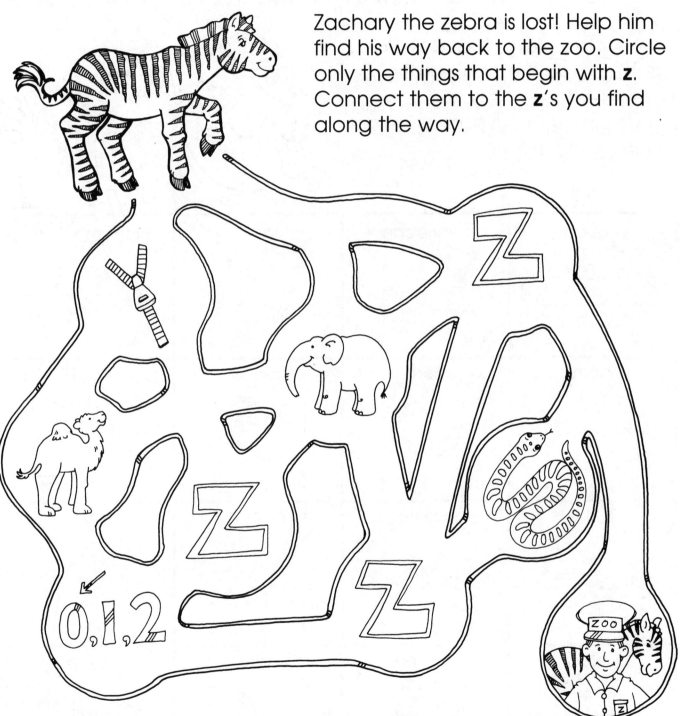

 What word begins with *z* **and sounds like a car speeding by very fast? (Hint: It rhymes with** *broom***.) On another sheet of paper, draw a race car. Think of a story to tell with your picture.**

City C and Country C

C *can make two sounds. If the vowels* **e** *or* **i** *come after the* **c**, *then* **c** *will have the* **s** *sound. If one of the other vowels (**a**, **o**, **u**) comes after the* **c**, *then* **c** *will have the* **k** *sound.*

Look at the pictures and words on this page. If it begins with an *s* sound, as in *city*, circle **s**. If it begins with a *k* sound, as in *country*, circle **k**.

couch	centipede	cow	cinnamon roll
k s	k s	k s	k s
corn	**cent**	**cereal**	**coat**
k s	k s	k s	k s
cake	**ceiling**	**cobra**	**cat**
k s	k s	k s	k s
celery	**coconut**	**circles**	**comb**
k s	k s	k s	k s

Use the words on page 22. Write each word that begins with the same sound as *city*.

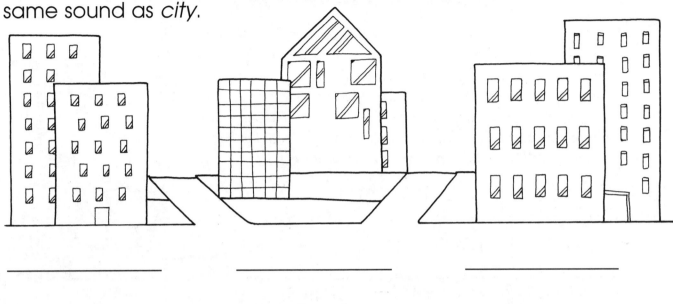

_____   _____   _____

_____

_____

Write each word that begins with the same sound as *country*.

_____   _____   _____

_____   _____   _____

 This word has two *c*'s in it. The first *c* sounds like an *s*. The other one sounds like a *k*. It is a fun place to see a show. There are clowns and elephants in a big tent. People do amazing tricks. What is it? On another sheet of paper, draw a picture of yourself doing a trick there.

Gary the Goat and George the Giraffe

G *can make two sounds. Usually, words that begin with* g *make the same sound that you hear in* **Gary** *and* **goat**. *But sometimes a* g *can sound like a* j, *as in* **George** *and* **giraffe**. *This usually happens when the vowels* e *or* i *come after the* g, *but not always. The best way to figure out which* g *sound to use is to try both sounds and see which one makes sense. For example, try saying* goat *with both* g *sounds. See? One of them does not make sense!*

Look at each picture below. If the picture begins like *goat*, circle **g**. If the picture begins like *giraffe*, circle **j**.

gate	girl	gingerbread man	gift
g — j	g — j	g — j	g — j

giant	guitar	gum	gerbil
g — j	g — j	g — j	g — j

goose	gorilla	general	gymnast
g — j	g — j	g — j	g — j

Use the words on page 24. Write each word that begins with the same sound as *Gary* on the goat.

Write each word that begins with the same sound as *George* on the giraffe.

 This word begins with a *g* that sounds like a *j*. It is a huge room. You can sit in the bleachers and watch a basketball game there. Most high schools have one. What is it? Think of another game that can be played there. On another sheet of paper, draw and color it.

Queen Q and Her Maidservant U

➡ **Q** *makes the sound you hear at the beginning of the word* **queen**.

Queen **Q** is very special. She has a maidservant named **U**. When Queen **Q** and Maidservant **U** work together, they make a sound that sounds like *kw*.

In each crown, write the word from the Word Box that matches the picture. (Hint: Do the easy ones first!)

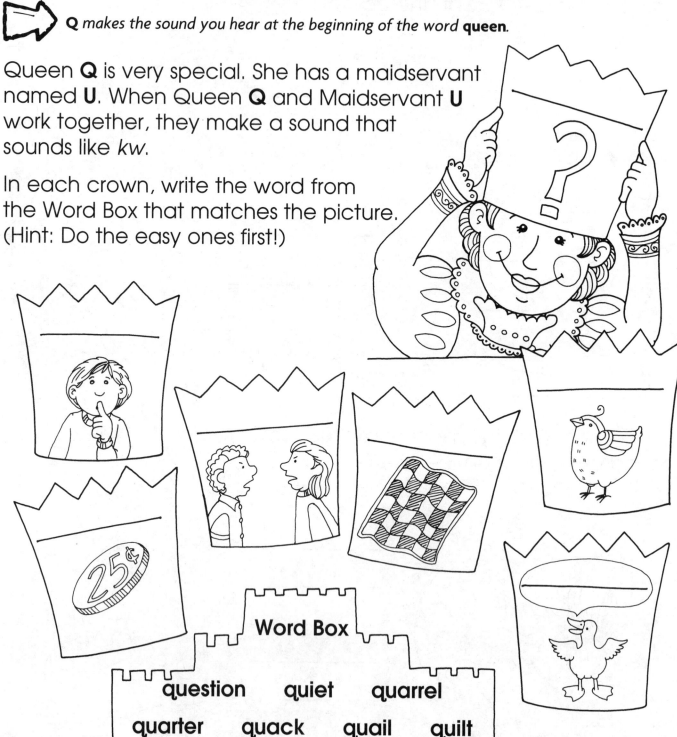

Word Box

question   quiet   quarrel

quarter   quack   quail   quilt

💡 **This word begins with *q*. Sometimes a teacher gives one to see if the students know their spelling words. It is another word for *test*. It rhymes with *Liz*. What is it? At playtime, pretend to be a teacher. Ask someone to be your student. Ask them questions. Then change places.**

Superhero X to the Rescue

X *makes the sound of* ks. *(Hint: Say the word* kiss *very fast!) Most of the time, an* **x** *is in the middle or at the end of a word.*

Help Superhero X put the missing **x** in each word. Then draw a line to the matching picture.

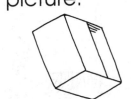

fo___

mi___er

ta___i

e___it

a___

si___

o___

bo___

e___ercise

tu___edo

It begins with *x*. It is a special kind of picture that a doctor takes so that she can see your bones. What is it? See if you can feel the bones in your fingers and hands. Make them wiggle!

Animal Tails

 Consonants can come at the beginning, middle, or end of a word. To help you hear the ending sound, say the word and stretch out the last sound. For example, when you see the picture of the bear, say "bear-r-r-r-r-r."

Say the name of each animal. Write the ending sound in the box by its tail.

 This creature lives in the sea. It does not have a tail. It has eight arms. Its head looks like a balloon. It ends with s. What is it? On another sheet of paper, draw one eating eight candy canes.

Name _____

Larry Last

Help Larry Last find the last sound that each word makes. Circle the correct letter under each lunchbox.

k   n   s

r   g   l

s   f   r

n   d   z

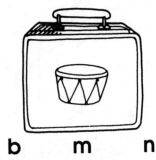

b   m   n

t   k   p

k   f   d

m   x   r

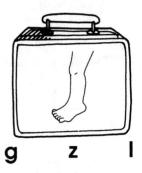

g   z   l

d   v   r

l   k   d

g   t   f

 You do this while you are asleep. It is like watching a movie in your head. It ends with _m_. What is it? On another sheet of paper, draw a picture about one that you have had. Tell about it.

Consonant Caboose

Find two words on each train that end with the same sound. Color them. Then write the letter of the ending sound in the caboose.

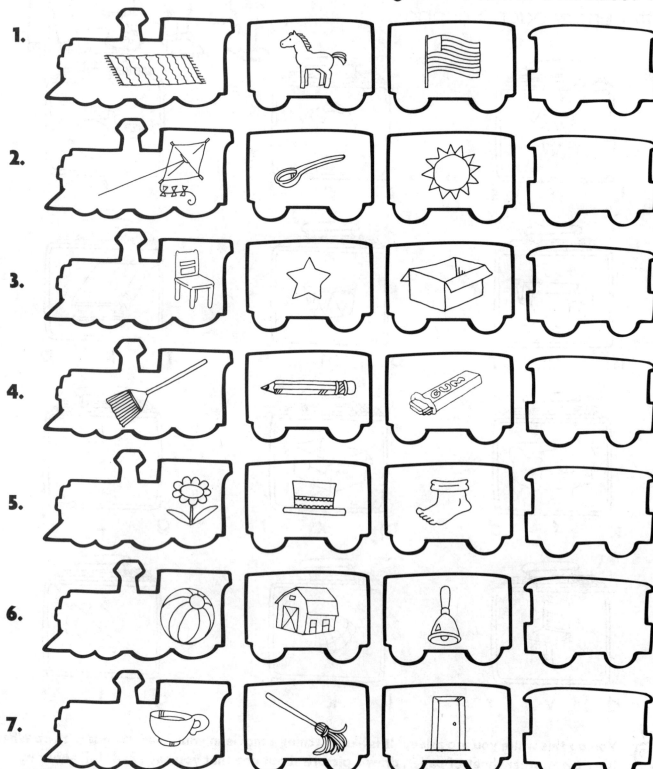

I Like the Middle!

Consonants can come at the beginning, middle, or end of a word. To help you hear the middle sound, say the word and pause for a second after you say the middle consonant. For example, when you see the picture below about magic, say "mag--ic."

Circle only the middle consonant in each word. Do not circle any vowels (*a, e, i, o, u*). Then draw a line to the picture that matches the word. The first one has been done for you.

1. magic

2. tulip

3. motor

4. fever

5. music

6. tiger

7. money

8. beaver

This stuff makes things sweet. It looks like white sand. Sometimes, you sprinkle it on your cereal. The word has a *g* in the middle. What is it? On another sheet of paper, draw five things that have this ingredient in them.

Name _____

Middle Man

Help Middle Man find the middle consonant in each word. Circle the correct letter under each mountain.

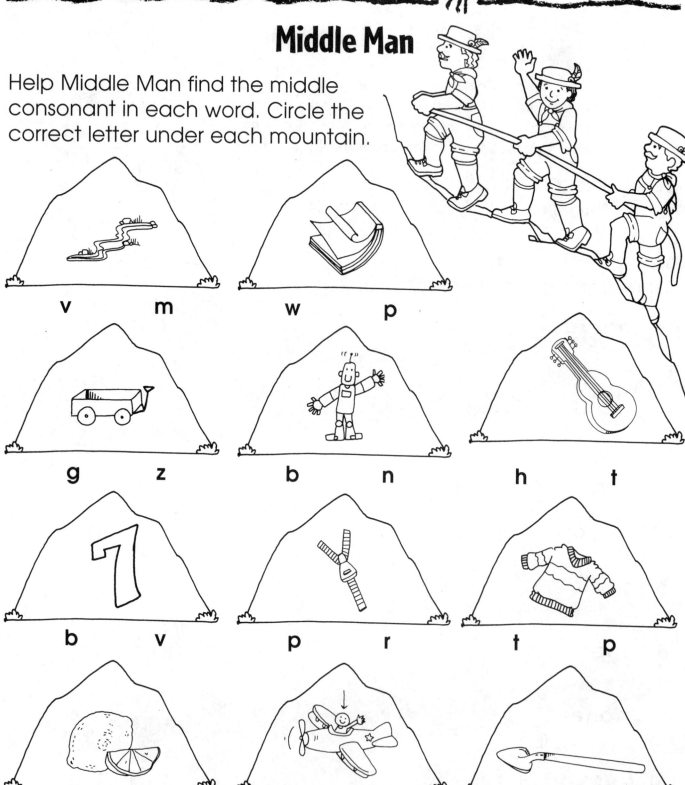

v   m

w   p

g   z

b   n

h   t

b   v

p   r

t   p

d   m

l   k

v   g

 This food looks like a doughnut. It is a kind of bread. Some people like to put cream cheese on it. The word has a *g* in the middle. What is it? On another sheet of paper, draw what you had for breakfast today.

Where Are They?

Draw a box around the middle consonant of each word in a star. Then circle each word in the puzzle. The words go across and down.

color

medal

baker

seven

f	c	o	r	d	e	f	w	a
g	s	n	m	i	l	i	a	m
s	a	s	e	v	e	n	t	e
e	l	t	v	e	o	a	e	d
b	a	k	e	r	m	l	r	a
a	d	c	o	l	o	r	a	l

water

salad

diver

final

 Nine of these circle the sun. Mars is one. Jupiter is one. Even Earth is one! The word has an *n* in the middle. What is it? On another sheet of paper, draw a make-believe planet and the people that live there.

Two Alike

Sometimes a word has double consonants in the middle of it. When that happens, you write it twice, but you only say it once.

Look at the picture in each bubble. Say the word. Write the missing letters.

ha___ ___y

pi___ ___ow

do___ ___ar

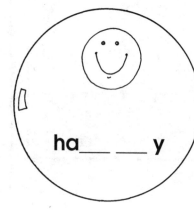
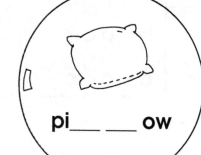

ri___ ___on

ha___ ___er

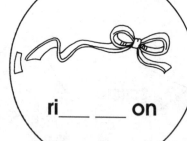

la___ ___er

bu___ ___on

ki___ ___ing

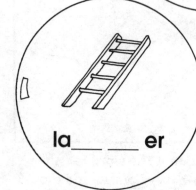

Double Trouble

Read to find out why these children got in trouble. Circle all the double consonants in each sentence. Then find the picture that goes with the sentence. Write the number of the sentence in the correct box.

1. William and Jesse giggled in class.

2. Emma and Jenna scribbled on the wall.

3. Hannah and Kelly tattled to Mommy.

4. Connor and Kenny held a muddy puppy.

Shhh! Consonants Sleeping!

Sometimes a consonant may make no sound at all. For example, when k and n come together, the k is silent. When w and r come together, the w is silent. When r and h come together, the h is silent.

Look at the words and pictures. Make a sleepy eye, like this,  above the consonant that is silent. Do not color it. Then color the other letters in the word.

knife

knot

knock

knit

wreck

write

wreath

wrist

rhinoceros

 This is part of your leg. It can bend. It starts with *kn*, but the *k* is silent. What is it?

More Sleeping Consonants

 Sometimes consonants in the middle or at the end of a word may make no sound at all. For example, when b *comes after* m, *the* b *is silent. When* n *comes after* m, *the* n *is silent. Sometimes when* g *and* h *come together, both letters are silent.*

Look at the words and pictures. Make a sleepy eye, like this, above the silent *b*, silent *n*, or silent *gh*. Do not color the silent letters. Color all the other letters.

comb

lamb

column

thumb

autumn

night

lightning

 This word has a silent *gh* in it. It is a word that describes the sun. It is why you cannot look at the sun. It rhymes with *fight*. What is it? Design a pair of really cool-looking sunglasses. On another sheet of paper, draw and color your design.

Word Puzzles

 Rhyming words *sound alike. They are made by changing only the beginning sound of a word. The rest of the word stays the same.*

Each word puzzle below shows how to make a rhyming word. The first one has been done for you.

1. man – m + f = __fan__

2. hook – h + b = _____

3.  cake – c + r = _____

4. dog – d + l = _____

5.  tire – t + f = _____

6.  well – w + b = _____

7. king – k + r = _____

 This word rhymes with *best.* **It is where baby birds hatch out of their eggs. What is it? On another sheet of paper, make a funny cartoon that shows something silly (not a bird) coming out of an egg.**

Be a Word Builder!

Make your own rhyming words. Look
at the picture and say the word.
Copy the word. Then change the first
letter using each of the letters on the
hammer to make new words.

p s r m f h b

h c m t w f

s l b

f j l h

cat

ball

dog

hand

 This word rhymes with *fish*. **It rhymes with** *dish*. **It is what you make when you blow out
the candles on your birthday cake! What is it? Draw yours on another sheet of paper.**

Mother Goose Rhymes

Poems are made with rhyming words. Read the Mother Goose rhymes. Find a rhyming word from the Word Box below to match each underlined word. Copy the word on the line.

1. Jack and <u>Jill</u>

Went up the _____

To fetch a pail of water.

Jack fell <u>down</u>

And broke his _____,

And Jill came tumbling after.

2. Hey diddle <u>diddle</u>

The cat and the _____,

The cow jumped

over the <u>moon</u>.

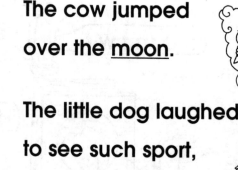

The little dog laughed

to see such sport,

And the dish ran

away with the _____.

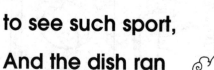

3. Hickory dickory <u>dock</u>

The mouse ran up the

_____.

The clock struck one,

The mouse ran down

Hickory dickory dock.

4. Mary had a little lamb,

Its fleece was white

as _____.

Everywhere that Mary went,

The lamb was sure to <u>go</u>.

Word Box					
fiddle	snow	crown	clock	hill	spoon

 This word rhymes with *corn*. It is something that Little Boy Blue could blow. It begins with *h*. What is it? Say as many Mother Goose rhymes as you know. On another sheet of paper, draw a picture of your favorite one.

Silly Sentences

Read each silly sentence. Circle the beginning consonant in each word. Then write the number of the sentence next to the picture that matches it.

1. Fox found four furry fish.

2. Rabbits run relay races.

3. Bees buzz by bananas.

4. Pink pigs peel potatoes.

5. Lion loves lizard lollipops.

6. Holly Hippo hangs her hats.

 Try to say these tongue twisters very fast:
Sister Susie's sewing socks for soldiers. Peter Piper picked a peck of pickled peppers.

Freda's Freckles

Help Freda solve each riddle below. Connect the freckles in alphabetical order to find the answer.

1. It has teeth, but it cannot bite. It begins with *s*. What is it?

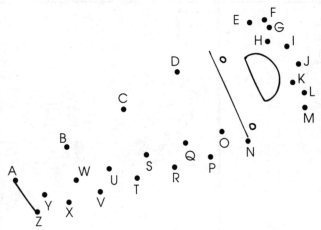

2. It has a trunk, but it is not an animal. It begins with *c*. What is it?

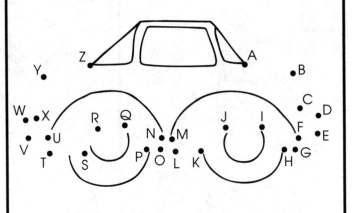

3. It is inside a pen, but it is not ink. It begins with *p*. What is it?

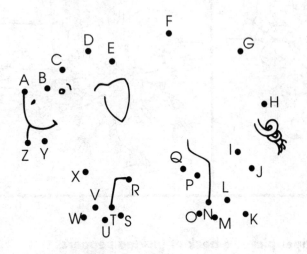

4. It has a face and two hands, but it is not a person. It begins with *w*. What is it?

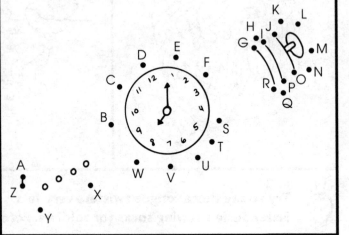

Name _____

Weather Words

Use the consonant clues to write the correct weather word in the puzzle.

sunny   rain   icicle   cloud

lightning   snowman   tornado

Across

3. It has two *c*'s. One sounds like an *s*. The other one sounds like a *k*.

4. It begins with *t*.

6. It is one word made from two words.

7. It has double consonants in the middle.

Down

1. It has a silent *gh* in it.

2. It ends with *d*.

5. It ends with *n*.

This storm is the biggest storm of all. It has fast wind and heavy rain. When it hits the coast, houses and trees are blown down. It begins with *h*. What is it? On another sheet of paper, draw a picture of this storm and make up a story to go with it.

Hidden Picture

Say the pictures in the puzzle.

Color words that begin with _t_ 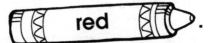 red .

Color words that begin with _b_  yellow .

Color words that begin with _s_ 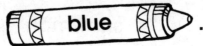 blue .

Color words that begin with _d_  black .

 This vessel begins with _s_. It floats on the water. The wind blows it along. It is in the puzzle above. What is it? On another sheet of paper, draw a beautiful island where this could take you.

What Have You Learned?

Look at the letter in each box. Say the picture. If the letter comes at the beginning of the word, copy it in the first box. If it comes in the middle of the word, copy it in the middle box. If it comes at the end of the word, copy it in the last box.

m	g	q	g	t	p
b	n	c	s	j	t
s	r	k	v	f	m
b	d	r	z	l	x
w	g	k	v	d	h

 This word begins with *y* and has a *y* in the middle, too! It is a toy. You wrap the string around your finger, and the toy goes up and down. What is it? On another sheet of paper, draw or write a list of your favorite toys.

Show What You Know!

Circle the sound that the **c** or **g** makes.

1. cup   k   s
2. celery   k   s
3. candle   k   s
4. giraffe   g   j
5. gerbil   g   j
6. gum   g   j

Draw lines to match the words to the pictures.

1. X-ray
2. quilt
3. taxi
4. question
5. six
6. queen

Fill in the blanks with the missing double consonants.

1. ra___ ___it
2. la___ ___er
3. pe___ ___y
4. a___ ___le
5. le___ ___er
6. fo___ ___il

Draw lines to match the words to the pictures.

1. write
2. knee
3. rhinoceros
4. comb
5. autumn
6. night

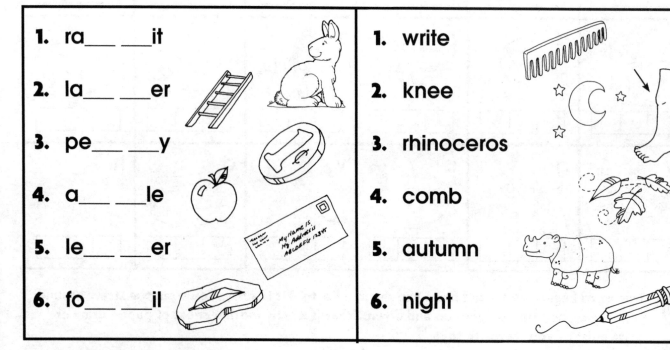

Page 5
bird, ball; belt, boat; banana, basket, bell, books; boots, bat; bee

Page 6
dog, duck, domino, dollar, dice, deer, dinosaur, door; dentist

Page 7
fan, fox, five, fork, football, feather, four; firefighter

Page 8
horn, house; helicopter, hammer; hand; heart, horse, hose; hat, hamburger, hanger; hide-and-seek

Page 9
jeans, jar of jelly; jump rope, jack-o'-lantern; jack-in-the-box, jacket; jelly beans

Page 10

kid

Page 11
lamp, lace, leaf, ladder; ladybug, lake, lamb, leg; lightning, lemon, letter, lettuce; lips, lizard, lobster, log; love

Page 12
motorcycle, milk, mop, mirror, mouse, mitten, monkey, moon, money; Mother or Mom

Page 13
nose, nine, needle, nail, nuts, net, necklace; newspaper

Page 14
popcorn, pineapple, porcupine, penguin, policeman, puppet, pencil, paper; penny

Page 15
rest, run, ride; rock, rake, roll; read, rope, rip; row, race, rush; rocket

Page 16

sandwich

Page 17
tiger, turtle; teapot (and teacup), toast (toaster); telephone, television; table, tape; tent

Page 18
vase, vegetables, violin, vest, vacuum, valentine; volcano

Page 19
Willy, worm, wanted, watermelon, window, wagon, wiggled, wall, wow, was, wonderful

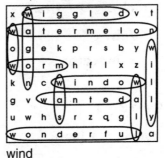

wind

Page 20

yes

Page 21

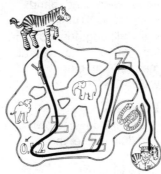

zoom

Page 22
couch—k, centipede—s, cow—k, cinnamon roll—s; corn—k, cent—s, cereal—s, coat—k; cake—k, ceiling—s, cobra—k, cat—k; celery—s, coconut—k, circles—s, comb—k

Page 23
city: centipede, cinnamon roll, cent, cereal, ceiling, celery, circles; country: couch, cow, corn, coat, cake, cobra, cat, coconut, comb; circus

Page 24
gate—g, girl—g, gingerbread man—j, gift—g; giant—j, guitar—g, gum—g, gerbil—j; goose—g, gorilla—g, general—j, gymnast—j

Page 25
Goat: gate, girl, gift, guitar, gum, goose, gorilla; Giraffe: gingerbread man, giant, gerbil, general, gymnast; gym or gymnasium

Page 26
question, quiet, quarrel, quilt, quail, quarter, quack; quiz

Page 27

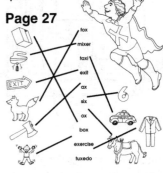

X-ray

Page 28

octopus

Page 29
n, l, r; n, m, k; d, x, g; r, l, f;
dream

Page 30
1. rug, flag—g; 2. spoon, sun—n; 3. chair, star—r;
4. broom, gum—m;
5. hat, foot—t; 6. ball, bell—l; 7. cup, mop—p

Page 31

1. magic
2. tulip
3. motor
4. fever
5. music
6. tiger
7. money
8. beaver

sugar

Page 32
v, p; g, b, t; v, p, t; m, l, v;
bagel

Page 33
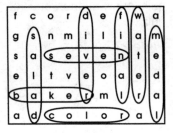

planet

Page 34
happy, pillow, dollar; ribbon, hammer; ladder, button, kissing

Page 35
1. William, Jesse, giggled, class; 2. Emma, Jenna, scribbled, wall; 3. Hannah, Kelly, tattled, Mommy;
4. Connor, Kenny, muddy, puppy; 3, 2, 4, 1

Page 36

knife   knot
knock   knit
wreck   write
wreath   wrist
rhinoceros

knee

Page 37

comb   lamb
column   thumb
autumn   night
lightning

bright

Page 38
1. fan; 2. book; 3. rake;
4. log; 5. fire; 6. bell;
7. ring;
nest

Page 39
hand: sand, land, band; ball: hall, call, mall, tall, wall, fall; dog: fog, bog, log, hog; cat: pat, sat, rat, mat, fat, hat, bat;
wish

Page 40
1. Jill–hill, down–crown;
2. diddle–fiddle, moon–spoon;
3. dock–clock;
4. snow–go;
horn

Page 41
3, 6, 4, 5, 2, 1

Page 42
Check children's dot-to-dot puzzles.

Page 43
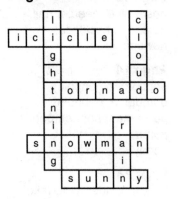

hurricane

Page 44
red: ten, tiger; yellow: baby, barn; blue: sun, soap, sock, sandwich; black: door, dog, dinosaur, duck, dime, die, doctor, donkey;
sailboat

Page 45
m—first, g—middle, q—first, g—last, t—middle, p—first; b—first, n—last, c—first, s—middle, j—first, t—last; s—first, r—middle, k—first, v—middle, f—first, m—last; b—middle, d—first, r—last, z—first, l—last, x—last; w—first, g—last, k—last, v—middle, d—last, h—first;
yo-yo

Page 46
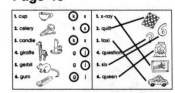

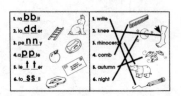